*A mother is not a person
to lean on but a person to
make leaning unnecessary.*

Dorothy Canfield Fisher

101 ways to be a great mom

Vicki Kuyper

Brentwood, Tennessee

101 Ways to Be a Great Mom
Copyright © 2005 by GRQ, Inc.

ISBN 1-59475-040-8

Published by Blue Sky Ink
Brentwood, Tennessee.

Editor: Lila Empson
Cover and Text Design: Whisner Design Group

05 06 07 4 3 2 1

*In praising or loving
a child, we love and
praise not that which
is, but that which
we hope for.*

Johann Wolfgang
von Goethe

Contents

Contents continued...

Introduction

In your busy life as a mom, you have to make every moment count. *101 Ways to Be a Great Mom* offers bite-size portions of insightful advice, practical tips, and creative activities designed to help you succeed in the most important job you'll ever have.

Whether it's making mealtime more fun, confronting conflict head-on, or joining your kids in finding out more about who God really is, each new day provides countless opportunities to grow right along with your kids. May *101 Ways to Be a Great Mom* inspire you to grab hold of these moments and transform them into positive memories—as God transforms you into the great mom he designed you to be.

The loveliest masterpiece of
the heart of God is the heart of
a mother.

Saint Thérèse of Lisieux

*Children are a blessing
and a gift from the LORD.*

Psalm 127:3 CEV

#1

Walk a Mile in Your Children's Sneakers

Think back, way back to when you were your children's age. Ponder what was most significant in your life. What did you long for? What did you fear? What fired up your emotions or calmed your heart?

Obviously, children experience the world in a different way than adults do. As a mom, the more you're able to put yourself in your children's shoes, the easier it will be to authentically connect with what they're going through. Empathizing with your children's joys and sorrows on a deeper level prolongs your patience and expands your insight, making you better able to meet their immediate needs in a godly way.

walk

Rejoice with those who rejoice, and weep with those who weep.

Romans 12:15 NKJV

>> While looking through old photo albums, reminisce about your childhood. During this quiet time, ask God to help you better understand your own children through what you recall about yourself.

#2

Get on the Floor

> *One laugh of a child will make the holiest day more sacred still.*
>
> Robert G. Ingersoll

floor

To share God's love, Jesus connected with people where they lived, worked, and played, whether at a wedding reception, by the village well, or around the dinner table. To better connect with your children, follow Jesus' example.

Venture into your children's world. Sit on the floor. Play in the sandbox. Chat with your children eye to eye. Although getting up off the floor may not be as easy as it was when you were your children's age, getting down to their level is an excellent way to rediscover the joy of imaginative play and to get better acquainted with the unique individuals God has created them to be.

≫ Make a habit of getting down on the floor at least once a day, engaging yourself in whatever your children are interested in at the time.

#3

Cultivate Quiet Moments

Do your children a favor. Help them become comfortable with silence. Bombarded with an almost constant cacophony of cell phones, video games, television programs, car stereos, and toys that talk, squawk, wail, and buzz, children as well as adults need the peace that's found in quiet.

Jesus regularly retreated into the wilderness. You and your family can make your home a wilderness amid the wildness of modern life. Designate a daily quiet time, when everyone engages in silent endeavors such as reading, writing, putting together a puzzle, or simply spending time with God.

quiet

Be still, and know that I am God.
Psalm 46:10 NIV

≫ When you're riding in the car, take a quiet break by turning off the radio, ceasing the conversation, and simply looking out the window, appreciating the world God made.

#4

Make Your Home Child-Friendly

> *Happiness is to be found only in the home where God is loved and honored, where each one loves, and helps, and cares for the others.*
>
> Theophane Vénard

home

Get to know your children and their friends even better by making your house the "place to be." Set aside a room or corner of your home where children can congregate with the amount of privacy that befits their age.

Place a variety of toys, games, and DVDs on child-accessible shelves. (Thrift stores are a great resource for changing this mix every so often.) Don't forget to keep a few quick-to-fix, healthy treats on hand that children can consume in their special place with a minimum of mess. Make every guest, big or small, feel welcome and at home.

>> Help your children and their friends practice responsibility: Ten minutes before guests are scheduled to leave, help guide them in getting the play area back in order.

#5

Celebrate the Little Things

Each new day, fresh from the hand of God, is worth celebrating. There's joy to be found even in small, unexpected places. Get into the habit of joining together as a family to celebrate the little things in life—the first snowflake, the last day of school, a power outage, a special act of kindness between siblings, or perseverance through a tough time.

Celebrations don't have to be expensive or stress-inducing. They can be as simple as a picnic by the fireplace during a thunderstorm or a hurrah-for-you note tucked in your child's lunchbox. The key is making memories you can share.

celebrate

This is GOD's work. We rub our eyes — we can hardly believe it! This is the very day GOD acted — let's celebrate and be festive!

Psalm 118:23–24
MSG

≫ Hold a just-because party at the dinner table. Give each member of your family a small gift, such as a handmade card or chocolate kiss, just because you love them.

#6

Support Your Children with Prayer

> *A mother's prayers, silent and gentle, can never miss the road to the throne of all bounty.*
>
> Henry Ward Beecher

prayer

As your children learn to walk, you support them with a strong, steady hand. Through prayer, you put your children in God's hands, which is a way of supporting them every step of the way, every day of their lives.

Prayer is a way of loving your children—as well as acknowledging that God's love for them is even deeper than your own. Turn every hope and fear you have for your family into a prayer. Then relax and be the mother God created you to be. Your children's heavenly Father is at work, even when you're asleep.

≫ Use driving time as prayer time for your children. When you put the key in the ignition, remind yourself that the key to your children's future is found in God.

#7

Say "I'm Sorry"

Big or small, everyone blows it now and then. A mom who can acknowledge her own failings, apologize to those she's hurt, forgive herself, and then move on is a mom who models humility and the frailty of humanity for her children.

Righting a wrong takes more than just muttering "Sorry" under your breath. It takes admitting what you did, voicing a sincere apology, asking anyone you've offended to forgive you, and making restitution, if necessary. When you apologize to your children, or your children witness you apologizing to your spouse or a friend, you help give them the courage to do the same.

sorry

> *Be kind to one another, tender-hearted, forgiving one another, even as God in Christ forgave you.*
>
> Ephesians 4:32
> NKJV

≫ When you apologize to your children, get down to their level and look them in the eye. Always end your apology with an "I love you."

#8

Learn from Your Little Ones

> *Who cannot find God in the heart of a child will never know him within cathedral walls.*
>
> Author Unknown

learn

Some of the world's best teachers aren't even old enough to attend school themselves. You can learn many lessons from your children, lessons such as the wonder found in a common ant or the fun it is to ride a swing. Sometimes "why" can be answered only by God.

To learn from a teacher of any age, you need to be an attentive student. Watch how your children interact with the world around them. Tune in to them when they talk, even if they talk a lot. Ask them questions. Give them ample opportunities to explore. Encourage them to try new things. And try new things yourself.

≫ Write down some of the lessons your children teach you. What you've written could make a great baby gift when grandchildren come along.

#9

Follow in Higher Footsteps

One way children learn is by imitating their parents. As God's child, you have a perfect Parent, one whose love never fails and whose patience never ends. There is no better example to follow than that of your heavenly Father.

Though Jesus never had children, you can better understand God's love for his children by reading about how Jesus loved the people God put in his care. Pick up a Bible and read the book of John. Notice how Jesus responded to interruptions, how he used everyday life as a teaching tool, how he humbly washed the disciples' feet. Consider what aspects of Jesus' life you can apply to your own.

follow

Be imitators of God, therefore, as dearly loved children.

Ephesians 5:1 NIV

≫ Choose one verse from the book of John that inspires you to be a better mom. Read that verse every morning for the next month, acting on what you learn.

#10

Forget Perfection

> Children have more
> need of models than
> of critics.
>
> Joseph Joubert

forget

Great moms are not perfect moms. They're women who are ordinary who trust God, who is extraordinary.

Great moms don't try to hide their mistakes or pass the blame to keep up appearances. They don't expect their children to be perfect so that their behavior will reflect well on their own parenting skills. They still answer the door to unexpected company, even when the house isn't spotless. They're women who risk greatness by risking failure and who are honest with themselves and others about both their victories and their defeats. They're women just like you, committed to being exactly who God created them to be.

≫ The next time your children make a mistake, share openly about a time when your humanness was as obvious as theirs is now. Remind them that only God is perfect.

#11

Love Your Children's Dad

Being a great mom is important, but it's no more important than being a great wife. The more your children witness a loving and respectful relationship between you and your husband, the more secure they'll feel.

Motherhood can be both tiring and time-consuming. However, that shouldn't put your marriage relationship on hold for the next eighteen years. Schedule regular date nights. They don't have to be elaborate or expensive. You don't even have to leave home, if you can find some privacy. Just be sure to spend time talking about you as a couple, instead of just about you as parents.

love

Love never gives up, never loses faith, is always hopeful, and endures through every circumstance.

1 Corinthians 13:7
NLT

>> Invite your children to help you make a date with your spouse. Ask for their help in deciding what you'll do as a couple—right down to what you'll wear.

#12

Brag a Little

> *Children are likely to live up to what you believe of them.*
>
> Lady Bird Johnson

brag

Every great mom should believe her children are special. (God believes that about you!) One way to remind your children of how special they are is to say positive things about them in front of others, including when they are likely to eavesdrop.

You don't need to go overboard, boasting about your children's superiority over more average children. You simply need to reinforce how proud you are of your children, in both big things and small. Even God said about Jesus, so others could hear, "This is My beloved Son, in whom I am well pleased" (Matthew 3:17 NKJV).

≫ Today, praise each of your children individually at least three times.

#13

Practice Being Present

Zombies should inhabit horror movies, not households. Unfortunately, when you find yourself overstressed, overscheduled, or overtired, it's easy to slip into playing the part of mom while your heart and mind feel almost dead to what's going on around you.

Being there physically for your children is important. However, unless you're there mentally as well, both you and your children are going to miss a lot of living and loving. Make the most of the moment at hand. Wherever you are, be all there—playing with your children, snuggling with your spouse, cleaning the garage, praying to God, or relaxing in the tub.

present

Be alert, be present. I'm about to do something brand-new.

Isaiah 43:19 MSG

>> Tonight during dinner, chat, chew slowly, and enjoy God's tasty provision. Refuse to multitask by watching television, trying to solve problems, reading the paper, or talking on the phone.

#14

Put Yourself in Time-Out

> *Jesus knows we must come apart and rest awhile, or else we may just plain come apart.*
>
> Vance Havner

time-out

Motherhood is a job with no quitting time. Even when you fall into bed at night, you can still be called into action at 2:00 a.m. A schedule like this needs the healthy balance of some time out.

A time-out needs to be more than just five minutes alone with the bathroom door closed. It should be a full morning, afternoon, or even twenty-four hours of doing something you truly enjoy. Scrapbook. Paint. Have a slumber party with a friend. Take a sack lunch and a good book to the park—without visiting the playground. Relax, journal, nap. Both you and your children will be glad you did.

>> Sit down with your spouse and schedule a time-out for yourself sometime during the next month.

#15

Listen More Than You Talk

Remember when your children spoke their first words? Memorable, wasn't it? Now ask yourself how much you remember of what your children said today. Not every word that comes out of your children's mouths is worth recording for posterity, of course. But you'll never know unless you listen.

As much as is possible, look your children in the eye when they speak. Don't cut them off or finish their sentences. Rely more on asking questions than giving lectures, to teach as well as to discipline. Listen with your eyes and heart, not just your ears. Remember, your children learn to listen through your example.

listen

> *Be quick to listen, slow to speak, and slow to get angry.*
>
> **James 1:19** NLT

≫ The next time your children ask lots of questions, they may want your attention more than they want an answer. Be gracious in giving it to them.

ponder

101 ways to

empathize

venture

engage

celebrate

be a great mom

relax

apologize

watch

#16

Make a Mess

No fragments of cookies or cake, no traces of frolicsome play, the heartstrings of motherhood break when the house keeps in order all day.

Harry Edward Mills

mess

Children are little scientists. They want to touch, taste, stack, sift, throw, or squish whatever they get their hands on so they can find out what happens. This can be a messy endeavor. Once you accept that fact, there's only one thing left to do. Forget about making the cover of *House Beautiful,* and join in the fun.

Help corral the chaos by setting up a specific area where children can experiment and stay involved in the process. When it's time to clean up, keep your own attitude positive. Help your children understand that choosing to make a mess means choosing to clean one up.

>> Tonight, turn dinner cleanup time into a game. Clear the table by carefully carrying "patients" to the dishwasher "hospital." Patients go home when dishes are put away.

#17

Be Full of Surprises

Every morning, the sun rises. But how it's going to rise—painting morning clouds raspberry red or perhaps hiding behind a drape of fog—is a surprise. That's just the way God works. He's consistent in what really matters, yet often unpredictable in his ways.

A great mom is a bit like God in that aspect. Her children know they can depend on her love and provision. Her creativity, however, sweetens life with the unexpected. So make burgers in fun shapes. Sing a silly song in the grocery store. Hide a new book under your children's pillows now and then. Keep your children guessing.

surprise

> *Surprise us with love at daybreak; then we'll skip and dance all the day long.*
>
> Psalm 90:14 MSG

≫ Surprise your children one Saturday morning by whisking them out of bed to a secret weekend destination. Have their bags packed and the camera ready.

#18

Talk About the Tough Stuff

> *The mother's heart is the child's schoolroom.*
>
> Henry Ward Beecher

talk

The tough stuff of life gets tougher as children get older. Often, so does talking about it. The best way to keep the lines of communication open—with toddlers through the teen years and beyond—is to be honest and forthright from the very beginning.

When your children ask questions about complex topics such as death, drugs, sex, or God, don't brush them off with a "wait until you're older" message. Remember what you were like at their age. Ask why they're interested. See what they know already. Correct any inaccuracies they believe. Then ask God to help you share your heart in a way that appropriately educates theirs.

≫ Keep your eyes open for children's books that deal with delicate issues. Add a few to your library to have on hand to share when the time is right.

#19

Keep Your Promises

There's an old adage that says "Promises are made to be broken." Nothing could be farther from God's truth. When God says he'll do something, he does it—and he asks his children to follow his example.

Whether it's the promise of going to the circus or of being punished for breaking a family rule, the truth behind your words will be measured by your follow-through. Take a moment to think before you speak. Say what you know to be true, not what you hope will happen. Then keep your word, just as God keeps his.

keep

> *For as many as are the promises of God, in [Jesus] they are yes.*
>
> 2 Corinthians 1:20
> NASB

>> If you have to break a promise to your children, apologize, and then evaluate why you couldn't keep your word, making sure it was an exception and not a pattern.

#20

Say "I Love You"

> *To love another person is to help them love God.*
>
> Sören Kierkegaard

say

You can show your children you love them in many ways—by making them lunch, washing their clothes, praying with them before bedtime, holding them close when their tears start to fall. However, you need to express love in words as well as actions.

A simple "I love you" is a declaration that doesn't become cliché, even if repeated frequently. You can add even more power to those three little words by telling your children *why* you—and God—love them. Help them to appreciate the lovable qualities God has woven into each one of them as well as to recognize that you love them just because they're yours.

>> Tell your children at unexpected moments that you love them. This includes when their present actions are not particularly lovable.

#21

Make Mealtimes Fun

Presentation is important at fine restaurants. The family dinner table shouldn't be any different. It takes only a moment or two to transform old family favorites into something new that will delight your children and encourage picky eaters.

Make a smiling face out of the food you put on your children's plates. Cut sandwiches into shapes with cookie cutters. Eat with your fingers—even if it's spaghetti. (You may want to provide bibs for the whole family!) Have a picnic by the fireplace. Add a bit of food color to the mashed potatoes. Let your children choose the menu and help prepare the meal.

fun

When you eat or drink or do anything else, always do it to honor God.

1 Corinthians 10:31
CEV

≫ Make eating leftovers fun. Listing leftovers on hand, print a menu of *Tonight's Specials.* Take orders early in the day so you can heat up only what's needed.

#22

Get Outside

> *Nature is God's greatest evangelist.*
>
> Jonathan Edwards

outside

Nature is filled with toys that don't require electrical cords: trees to climb, flowers to sniff, dirt to dig in, and sand to sift. Nature, God's perfect playground, invites families to hike, wade, explore, and more. Yet, nature is more than a playground. It's also a silent sermon. Lightning speaks of God's power. Butterflies praise his creativity. Wildflowers whisper that God cares about the details.

Join your children in looking for the Creator's fingerprints in all he's created. Use nature as a teaching tool, a catalyst to spark spiritual questions and provide you with opportunities to help your children better understand God.

≫ Don't let bad weather keep you indoors. Dress appropriately and head out with the children for a brief walk in the rain or for a snowman-making contest in the snow.

#23

Watch Your Words

Words have power. You can use them to order a sandwich, teach physics, or break a child's heart. Every time you open your mouth, you choose how you will use your verbal power. Habit may make you less aware of each individual word choice. However, the choice and the responsibility remain solely yours.

Throughout the Bible, God encourages you to use your words wisely and well. Every day, what you say as a mom (and how you say it) has a tremendous impact on your children. If you're in the habit of saying whatever pops into your head, slow down. Think before you speak.

words

A man has joy in an apt answer, and how delightful is a timely word!

Proverbs 15:23
NASB

>> Today, make a conscious effort to listen to what comes out of your mouth. Ask yourself if your words are as loving as you would like them to be.

#24

Laugh 'Til Your Stomach Hurts

> *A good laugh is sun-shine in a house.*
>
> William Makepeace
> Thackeray

laugh

One thing you don't have to teach your children is how to laugh. It's a crazy little response mechanism God incorporated into the human body. Some adults tend to squelch this urge as they mature. But great moms don't lose their sense of humor. With their children's help, moms nurture it.

Share jokes around the dinner table. Tickle your children during commercials while watching television. Relieve stress by watching a funny family film. Do something downright silly, just for your children's benefit. Read humorous cards together at the grocery store. Laugh with your children, and don't be afraid to laugh at yourself.

>> Every week, read the comic strips in the Sunday paper together as a family.

#25

Be the Grownup

Throwing tantrums, showing off, and being unwilling to share are just a few of the childish tendencies moms often have to face in their own lives. It's true that becoming an adult happens naturally. Acting like one, however, takes both God's help and personal perseverance.

To be the kind of mom your children can look up to and learn from, you need to continue to mature every day of your life. There's always some area you can grow up in. Consider how you react when nothing goes right and time is running out. Are you calm or out of sorts? Just look to the life of Jesus to see how a balanced, loving adult acts. Then imitate his ways.

grownup

> *Let the wonderful kindness and the understanding that come from our Lord and Savior Jesus Christ help you to keep on growing.*
>
> 2 Peter 3:18 CEV

>> Ask God to reveal to you any areas of immaturity you need to address in your own life.

#26

Know Your Children's Friends

*We are shaped
and fashioned by
what we love.*

Johann Wolfgang
von Goethe

know

You're careful to teach your children right from wrong, and you are careful to be an example you'd be proud for them to follow. You're not your children's only teacher, though. Your children's friends influence your children every time they're together.

While you can set some limits on whom your children spend time with and what they do together, it's not your job to handpick their friends. The best way to guide your children toward positive relationships is by getting to know and love their friends. The more your children's friends sense your genuine concern for them, the less they'll be tempted to do anything you'd disapprove of.

>> When your children make new friends, invite them and their parents for some informal fun together as a family.

#27

Discipline with Love

Parenthood can be frustrating. Just ask God. Consider how well he's explained to his children the right thing to do, and yet his children frequently choose not to do it. But God doesn't give up; God loves his children. The same is true for you and your own children.

The exact methods you choose to encourage your children to go the right way, God's way, can be as diverse as the children themselves. However, if you discipline your children out of love rather than out of anger born of frustration, embarrassment, or impatience, then you're going God's way. You're choosing to be an obedient child—and a great mom.

love

> *Do not provoke your children to anger, but bring them up in the discipline and instruction of the Lord.*
>
> **Ephesians 6:4** NASB

≫ Anytime you feel angry with your children, stop and tell God about it. Pray silently or aloud with your children to help you discipline out of love instead of emotion.

#28

Forget Playing Favorites

In praising or loving a child, we love and praise not that which is, but that which we hope for.

Johann Wolfgang von Goethe

forget

Jesus' disciples, Mother Teresa, and Billy Graham are just a few people who are well-known for the good they've done in God's name. If God had a list of favorite people, certainly they would be on it. But love doesn't play favorites. God loves the convict who turns to him just as deeply as the martyr who dies for him.

Take a lesson from God. Relate to your children as individuals. Spend one-on-one time with each child. Learn to appreciate the singular beauty and wonder God has woven into each of them. Ask God to help you see them as he does.

≫ If one child is harder for you to connect with than another, pay attention to how you relate to him or her for one day. Act on what you observe.

#29

Count the Stars

Every evening, God puts his power and creativity on display in the heavens. Use God's visual aid of the night sky to help your children understand tough concepts such as infinity, eternity, and God's omnipresence.

Drive to a spot as far from city lights as possible. Place a blanket on the ground, snuggle close together, and try to count the stars. How high can you get? Remind your children that some stars can be viewed only from the other side of the world, while others are too distant for the human eye to see. Consider what that tells you about God.

count

He determines the number of the stars and calls them each by name. Great is our Lord and mighty in power; his understanding has no limit.

Psalm 147:4–5 NIV

≫ When a meteor shower is predicted to occur in your area, wake your children. An hour of lost sleep is worth a time of family togetherness and awe.

#30

Visit the Library

Books are not made for furniture, but there is nothing else that so beautifully furnishes a house.

Henry Ward Beecher

library

For family entertainment on a tight budget, nothing can beat the local library. Along with books on every imaginable subject, story times, and reading clubs, you can also borrow audio books to enjoy on road trips.

If your children feel at home in a library, their study habits will show it. But don't just drop the children off. Peruse the aisles yourself. Check out a book on parenting or mastering a new hobby. Find out why a book is a classic by reading it. Visiting the library together is one way to help children understand you're never too old to learn something new.

≫ Help your children become critical thinkers by asking what they enjoyed most and least about every book they have read.

#31

Ask for Help

help

Being a great mom is a group effort that begins with a solid dependence on God and is strengthened by a strong partnership with your spouse. It is further supported by your friends and church family. On occasion, however, great moms like you may also need to rely on professionals in the medical and mental health fields to help meet your needs and the needs of your family.

Utilizing valuable health resources and support systems takes humility. When you've come to the end of your rope, do more than just hold on. Reach out to others for the help you need.

> *If one person falls, the other can reach out and help. But people who are alone when they fall are in real trouble.*
>
> Ecclesiastes 4:10
> NLT

≫ The next time a friend offers to help, accept help gladly and gratefully.

corral

101 ways to

ask

correct

promise

express

be a great mom

transform

join

think

#32

Talk While You Walk

> *The art of teaching is the art of assisting discovery.*
>
> Mark Van Doren

talk

A walk around the block is good for your heart, both physically and emotionally. When you invite your children to join you, your walk becomes relationally beneficial as well. Just getting outside and enjoying God's wonderland of creation is a great conversation starter for you and your children, but don't stop there. Use this time to ask a thought-provoking question or two.

Walking next to someone, as opposed to conversing face-to-face with constant eye contact, often helps people open up more. Use this opportunity to ask questions such as "What do you like best about our family?" or "What would you like to ask God?"

≫ Make a list of talk-while-you-walk questions that you would like to ask your children.

#33

Choose Your Battles

As a mom, you're going to fight some honest-to-goodness life-and-death battles. These will include battles for your children's physical, mental, and spiritual health. Between these major battles, you'll be faced with countless minor skirmishes—what your children will or will not eat, how they'll wear their hair, how neat they'll keep their rooms.

In the big picture of life, skirmishes such as these don't amount to much. On inconsequential matters, allow your children freedom to make choices, even if their choices differ from yours. Save your immovable no for the battles with your children that you can't afford to lose.

choose

Point your kids in the right direction—when they're old they won't be lost.

Proverbs 22:6 MSG

>> The next time you're ready to turn down a child's request, talk about what it would take for you to say yes. See if you can work out a compromise.

#34

Look for Reasons to Say "Thanks"

> *Were there no God,*
> *we would be in this*
> *glorious world with*
> *grateful hearts, and*
> *no one to thank.*
>
> Christina Rossetti

thanks

You don't need the IRS to tell you that your children are dependents. Your children depend on you for food, shelter, transportation, guidance, you name it. They have so many reasons to be thankful for you. Your reasons for voicing gratitude toward them may be less obvious, but they are no less worthy of thanks.

When children are young and dependent on others for so much, words of gratitude are often reserved for times when they do what they're told. Be creative with your gratitude. Voice your thanks for their doing acts of kindness, for their making you laugh, or for their being who God created them to be.

≫ When your children do something extraordinarily thoughtful, go a step beyond the spoken word. Write a thank-you note and place it on their pillow.

#35

Downsize Your Family's Schedule

Dance classes, soccer practice, piano lessons, and church camping trips are opportunities for personal growth and fulfillment. Overstuffing your schedule is a little like overeating. What seems good at first loses its appeal and soon leaves you feeling lethargic and uncomfortable.

Determining when your day is full takes prayer and planning. Commit to only one or two weekly extracurricular activities for your children. Try to book only one evening during the weekend for social activities. Save plenty of room for family fun, relaxation, and the unexpected.

schedule

Teach us to number our days, that we may present to You a heart of wisdom.

Psalm 90:12 NASB

>> Review last week's family calendar. Compare the hours your family spent together with the hours your family spent in planned activities. If you see a change that needs to be made, make it.

#36

Try Something New

Normal day, let me be aware of the treasure you are.

Mary Jean Iron

n e w

When your daily routine begins to feel more like a rut, shake things up a bit. With your children, learn a new skill like juggling, snowboarding, yodeling, or origami. Learn to eat dinner with chopsticks. Learn how to chart direction from the stars. Head to a park across town you've never visited before. Allow your children to help decorate one wall of their room with water-based paint.

Stretch your creative muscles. Prove to your children that an old mom can learn new tricks. At the same time you're making memories, you'll be helping your children discover the joy of exploring God's wide world of possibilities.

>> Buy a box of Japanese candy wrapped in rice paper in the Asian section of your local market. Try it with your children. Discuss how it feels to eat paper.

#37

Turn Mistakes into Teaching Opportunities

Jonah was an Old Testament prophet with an attitude problem. God told him to go to Nineveh and tell the people to change their evil ways. But instead, Jonah headed the opposite direction. After God allowed Jonah to be swallowed by a great fish, Jonah reconsidered his decision and prayed for another chance. God gave it to him—and this time Jonah headed straight to Nineveh.

Everyone makes poor choices and mistakes. When your children fail, talk about what happened and why. Then give your children another chance. Helping your children apply what they've learned will help transform information into wisdom.

turn

Wisdom is a tree of life to those who embrace her; happy are those who hold her tightly.

Proverbs 3:18 NLT

>> Recall a mistake you made in the past and what you learned from it. Share the story with your children.

#38

Be Honest

> *Sweet is the smile of home; the mutual look when hearts are of each other sure.*
>
> John Keble

honest

Honesty is a character trait that pleases God because it reflects his own nature. You can give your children a flesh-and-blood example of what God is like by choosing to live your life in an honest and trustworthy manner.

Choose to pay your taxes right down to the lawful penny. Drive the speed limit. When you've been under-charged, return to the store to pay what you rightfully owe. Shun little white lies. Your honesty will not only please God and serve as a good example, it will also assure your children that you're a mom who is worthy of their trust.

>> Take a moment to thank God for his complete honesty with you and ask him to reveal to you any dishonest habits you may have in your own life.

#39

Take Vacations

A great vacation begins long before the family and luggage are loaded into the car. It starts well in advance with a dream, a budget, and careful planning. Consider what type of activity your family enjoys most. Review your available vacation time and mark your calendar—the earlier the better. Set aside money each month so that you can pay for your trip in cash when the time arrives.

If the budget is tight, don't overlook trading houses with a friend, camping, or taking a series of one-day mini-adventures right from home. The key is to enjoy family time apart from your day-to-day family routine.

vacation

God richly gives us everything to enjoy.
1 Timothy 6:17 NCV

>> Get your children involved in vacation planning. Let them each choose one activity the family can enjoy together during your trip, and plan one meal they'll help prepare.

#40

Put Safety First

> *The center of
> God's will is our
> only safety.*
>
> Betsie ten Boom

safety

Life is fragile. While it's true your children's physical well-being ultimately lies in God's hands, you still have a responsibility to care for your children's physical needs to the best of your ability. You need to provide them with a safe place to thrive.

That begins with helping them get in the habit of making safe choices, such as fastening seat belts, wearing bicycle helmets, crossing only on green lights, wearing sunscreen, and taking medication only when it's given to them by your doctor or a family member. Live what you teach. Do what you can. Trust God for what's out of your hands.

≫ With your children, act out what to do if they're accosted by a stranger. Emphasize this will probably never happen, but it's something that's good to know.

#41

Keep a Journal

There are so many details about your children's childhoods you'll want to remember—cute turns of phrase, silly antics, hard-earned accomplishments. When these potential memories happen, you'll feel certain you could never forget something so important.

journal

Fast-forward twenty years. Your baby is in college, and you're surprised at how many of those precious moments are not as clear as they once were. Take time today to preserve them. Jot down just a sentence or two when something memorable happens. You'll help preserve a legacy for your children that they'll enjoy hearing about when they're older.

O God, You have taught me from my youth; and to this day I declare Your wondrous works.

Psalm 71:17 NKJV

≫ Set aside one hour every month to add more detail to any of the notes you've jotted down in your journal about your children.

#42

Know Your Neighbors

> *I am to become a Christ to my neighbor and be for him what Christ is for me.*
>
> Martin Luther

k n o w

A neighborhood is more than the area you live in. It's also a community you develop. While frequent moves, hectic schedules, and electric garage door openers have all taken their toll on modern-day neighborhoods, that doesn't mean borrowing a cup of sugar from next door is old-fashioned. In fact, caring for your neighbors pleases God—while it teaches your children how to make friends.

To draw your neighborhood closer together, reach out. Get to know your neighbors' names. Personally deliver Christmas cards. Volunteer to watch your neighbors' house when they're on vacation. Bring them to God in prayer.

>> Bake a batch of cookies with your children. Have your children join you, going door-to-door to share the treats with those who live nearby, whether you've met before or not.

#43

Snack Healthy

healthy

Your grocery store's snack aisles display a tempting array of goodies to please every palate. Yet what your taste buds want and what your body needs can be two different things, especially when so many people have been raised in a culture of fast food and sugar overload.

Help your children discover how good healthy foods can be. Offer fresh fruit, yogurt, nuts, bite-size carrots, frozen fruit bars, ice water, and low-fat milk in place of chips, candy, cookies, and soda. Be an example to your children by eating when you're hungry, not when you're bored, and making wise, healthy choices.

> *God said, "Look! I have given you the seed-bearing plants throughout the earth and all the fruit trees for your food."*
>
> **Genesis 1:29** NLT

≫ Mix two cups each of dried fruit, nuts, and unsalted popcorn. Put individual servings in plastic sandwich bags so children can grab a healthy snack on the go.

#44

Make Chores Family-Friendly

> *A mother is not a person to lean on but a person to make leaning unnecessary.*
>
> Dorothy Canfield Fisher

chores

Chances are you don't consider vacuuming, cleaning the kitchen, and folding the laundry highlights of your week. Your children may regard household chores as distractions that get in the way of their free time.

Change the way you look at chores, and your family will follow suit. Treat household responsibilities as a hands-on lesson in servanthood. Combine chore time with prayer time. Pray for family members as you fold their clothes. Praise God for the gift of having whatever you're expending effort to maintain. Once a month, tackle a big chore as a family. Celebrate its completion in a special way.

≫ Do one of your children's chores for them. Leave a note explaining what you did and why—just because you love them. You may start a family tradition.

#45

Let Children Dress Themselves

God has a sense of style. He clothed wildflowers in brilliant hues, and he clothed wildlife in spots, stripes, and fabulous fur. Yet the outer shell God has given his glorious creations is simply a covering, a decoration devoid of deeper meaning.

Letting children dress themselves gives them an outlet to create in a similar way. Some children like to express themselves with color and may pair paisley with a floral print. Others simply grab whatever is handy. As long as your child's outfit doesn't dishonor God, it's not worth fighting over. Emphasize the beauty of who your children are instead of what they wear.

dress

All this time and money wasted on fashion — do you think it makes that much difference?

Matthew 6:28 MSG

≫ To save time and hassles in the morning, have your children lay out tomorrow's clothing the night before after a brief weather report from Mom.

#46
Spin a Globe

> *My soul weeps for the whole world.*
>
> Staretz Silouan

globe

You can give your children a glimpse of the world without blowing your travel budget. Pick up a globe or an atlas. Give it a spin or flip to a page, and begin to explore. The more your children know about the world, the more compassion they will have for people whose lives are different from their own.

Make world events a regular part of your family conversation. Read folk tales from different countries. Support a foreign missionary. Visit an international restaurant, or prepare an exotic dish. Before you eat, pray for the people who live in the country where your meal recipe originated.

≫ Check out a travel video or DVD from your library. Watch it together as a family and discuss how this foreign locale differs from where you live.

#47

Reach Out to Others

Your children can be God's hands and feet in this world. They can be living answers to prayer for people in need. The more generous you are with your time, talents, and resources, the more natural it will seem to your children to give of themselves.

Donate seldom-used clothes and toys to charity. Have your children join you in serving at a soup kitchen. Shovel snow for an elderly neighbor. Pray as a family for friends who are struggling with their health. Send a card to a lonely friend or relative. Your opportunities to serve others are as open as your eyes and your heart.

others

Never walk away from someone who deserves help; your hand is God's hand for that person.

Proverbs 3:27 MSG

≫ As a family, give financially to help children in need around the world or in your community. Involve your children by giving them the opportunity to contribute from their allowances.

walk

101 ways to

allow

plan

stretch

teach

be a great mom

choose

review

trust

#48

Think Outside the Box

*The only real voyage
of discovery consists
not in seeking new
landscapes but in
having new eyes.*

— Marcel Proust

think

Television can be a useful and entertaining tool for your family. All that's required is a little planning and self-control.

Be wise with television time. Decide what you're going to watch before you turn it on, instead of channel-surfing. Turn the television off as soon as the program's over. Watch another show or mute commercials so that you're not tempted to buy something you don't need. Discuss what God would like or dislike about what you watch. Let your children choose no more than one program to watch each day, keeping the television in a family area, not a bedroom. Enjoy television together in mod-

>> Keep the television off for one week and see what creative ways your family can come up with to spend your new free time.

#49

Catch Some ZZZs

To be a great mom, you need to do what you can to keep your body and mind in great shape. A good night's sleep is a simple way to help achieve your goal.

catch

If you're having trouble sleeping soundly, cut back on the caffeine, stick with a regular bedtime, and grab a fifteen-minute nap when necessary during the day. (More than fifteen minutes will make you feel tired.) Instead of watching television in bed, which actually wakes your mind up, sip a cup of hot milk, listen to soft music, and talk to God. Then lie back, close your eyes, and enjoy God's gift of rest.

> *I lay down and slept; I awoke, for the LORD sustains me.*
>
> Psalm 3:5 NASB

≫ At least a half-hour before bedtime, dim the lights. This will help your body prepare to fall asleep more quickly once you hit the sheets.

#50

Cuddle Up and Read

*There are perhaps
no days of our child-
hood we lived so fully
as those we believe
we left without
having lived them:
those we spent with
a favorite book.*

Marcel Proust

r e a d

Reading aloud to your children will help them learn to love reading and will improve their attention span and vocabulary. It can also help calm children down before bedtime. Best of all, it's a lot of fun.

Find a comfortable, well-lit spot to cuddle up together. Over time, work your way through a variety of titles. Let your children choose books from the library, and build a library of your own from garage sales and sales racks. Read your own childhood favorites aloud. As your children learn to read, let them read a portion of the book to the family. And when you're on the road, don't forget audio books.

>> To encourage your children's own storytelling skills, stop reading mid-chapter and have each child guess what will happen next.

#51

Let Your Children Fail

When your children first learn to tie their own shoes, it's easy to let them fail. After all, a few knots won't hurt anything. However, as they get older the consequences of failure often become more serious. Your children may alienate a friend, fail a class, or get into debt. At times like these, your loving mom's heart will long to untie the knots in your children's lives.

Before you do, ask God to help you know when to let natural consequences be their own tough teacher. That's the only teacher some children will listen to or learn from.

fail

> *Fear–of–GOD is a school in skilled living—first you learn humility, then you experience glory.*
>
> Proverbs 15:33 MSG

≫ When your children fail, pay attention to how you respond. Ask what God will teach you through this.

#52

Make Music Together

There is something exceedingly thrilling in the voices of children singing.

Henry Wadsworth
Longfellow

music

After God parted the Red Sea, allowing the Israelites to make it safely to the other side, Moses' followers celebrated their freedom with music. Moses' sister led the former captives in an original song, praising God for what he'd done.

Help your children feel free to do the same thing. Sing along with worship music while riding in the car. Encourage your children to learn to play a musical instrument. Learn a few chords on guitar so you can lead family sing-alongs. With the Psalms as a guide, try writing your own music as a gift to God and encourage your children to do the same.

>> Write a short thank-you song to God. Don't worry about rhyme or perfect pitch. Just sing what's in your heart. Share the song with your children.

#53

Join a Church Family

Your family is larger than the people who live in your house. It's even bigger than your ancestral family tree. According to God, your family includes every person who follows him.

Your spiritual family can be a source of friendship, encouragement, and support. Sharing your life, including your personal joys and struggles with motherhood, with those who share your faith can also help you draw closer to your heavenly Father. This is key to becoming the mom you want to be. The best place to connect is at a local church. If you're unsure of where to go, check out the websites of churches nearby.

join

> Be faithful, loving, and easy to get along with. Worship with people whose hearts are pure.
>
> 2 Timothy 2:22 CEV

≫ If you don't attend church regularly, visit one this Sunday as a family. If you're already part of a church family, reach out to a member you haven't yet met.

#54

Nurture Imagination

> *The soul without imagination is what an observatory would be without a telescope.*
>
> Henry Ward Beecher

imagine

A stick is just a stick, until a child picks it up. Then the power of imagination can transform it into a fishing pole, a sword, or a conductor's baton.

Children with vivid imaginations have an easier time entertaining themselves when they're young, and they are better equipped to become creative problem-solvers as adults.

Help your children develop their mind's eye by choosing toys that rely more on imagination than batteries. Save large cardboard boxes for building forts and castles. Play games like charades as a family. Nurture your own imagination by coming up with new ways to nurture theirs.

≫ Give your children old clothes from a thrift store or your closet. Ask them to dress up for dinner as someone other than themselves, staying in character throughout the meal.

#55

Make Holidays Memorable

Holidays should be happy days and family times that encourage laughter, love, and lots of memory-making. One way to accomplish this is to focus on *why* you're celebrating, instead of *how* you're celebrating. This will help you let go of some traditions that may be making your holidays more stressful.

How you choose to personalize your holidays is up to you. Perhaps you'll bake Jesus a birthday cake instead of making dozens of Christmas cookies, or maybe you'll eat rice and beans on Thanksgiving as a reminder of how much you have to be thankful for. Involve your family in the decisions. Enjoy your time together.

holidays

The godly are showered with blessings.

Proverbs 10:6 NLT

>> Instead of buying new clothes to wear this Easter, give the money you would have spent to a homeless shelter. Talk with your children about your new tradition.

#56
Waste Film

> *Each day of our lives we make deposits in the memory banks of our children.*
>
> Charles R. Swindoll

film

Children love looking at photos of themselves when they were babies, and so do their parents. Whether you choose to use video, 35mm prints, or digital technology, creating a visual record of your children's childhoods has never been easier. All you need is the equipment (even a disposable camera will do) and a commitment.

Take photos of major milestones and accomplishments. Snap impromptu shots at the dinner table. Catch the children while they're napping. Have them imitate animals at the zoo. Put the developed photos in albums or photo boxes so you can enjoy them for years to come.

>> Give each child a self-adhesive photo album. Pass on your discarded photos, double prints, or a few digital images to help them create their own memory books.

#57

Enjoy Dinner Together

Jesus shared much more than food with those he loved at the Last Supper. He also shared instruction and companionship. You can share these same things with your children around the dinner table each evening.

Making dinnertime family time becomes even more important as children get older. The busier a family's schedule gets, the less time everyone has to connect. Use your time together well. Let everyone share a highlight and a low point from their day. Ask questions. Respond to problems with mini life-lessons, and save disciplinary lectures for individual one-on-one time. Laugh a little, and don't forget to enjoy the food.

dinner

> *Give us the food we need for each day.*
> Matthew 6:11 NCV

≫ This week, have your family take turns praying after the meal, instead of before. Thank God for the food and ask for his help with any problems your family discussed.

#58

Try a New Recipe

The discovery of a new dish does more for the happiness of mankind than the discovery of a star.

Anthelme Brillat Savarin

recipe

When the Israelites wandered through the desert for forty years, meal planning for the family was a snap. Manna for breakfast. Manna for lunch. Manna for dinner. Although your grocery options are much more varied, it's easy to find yourself serving the same thing again and again out of convenience or habit.

Working new recipes, especially ones with unfamiliar ingredients, into your weekly menu can help prevent your children from becoming picky eaters. Serve one new dish along with familiar favorites. Ask each person to try at least two bites of everything served. Let your children help choose new recipes as well as prepare them.

≫ Check an international cookbook out of the library and prepare a new recipe as a family.

#59

Share

When it comes to sharing a favorite toy, children can have a tough time letting go, even momentarily, of what they see as theirs. Often, adults are no different. Consider how you'd feel if someone ate the last piece of cake you'd saved for yourself or asked to borrow your new car.

God asks his children to graciously share what he has graciously given. Helping your children learn to please God in this way begins by setting an example in your own life. If letting others borrow something you value makes you feel uncomfortable, ask God to help break the hold that possessiveness has on your heart.

s h a r e

In all things show yourself to be an example of good deeds, with purity in doctrine, dignified, sound in speech which is beyond reproach.

Titus 2:7–8 NASB

≫ Spend some time today praying about how you can more generously share what you have.

#60

Give Your Children Space

> *Home is the sacred refuge of our life.*
>
> John Dryden

space

In the Bible, the apostle Mark told of a time when the apostles were so busy taking care of others that they didn't have time to eat. Jesus responded by saying, "Come with me by yourselves to a quiet place and get some rest" (Mark 6:31 NIV).

As a mom, you know how important it is to have a quiet, private spot to retreat. Your children have that same need for a refuge. If your children share a room, give them each a separate space that is solely theirs. Even a cozy chair or a corner stacked with pillows will do.

≫ Make individual refuges for your children by cutting windows and doors in large cardboard boxes. Complete each retreat by adding pillows, a flashlight, and a couple of books.

#61

Look Without Labeling

Every child God creates is an individual. As your children grow, their individuality can lead you to label them, mentally if not verbally: the easy one, the slow one, the messy one, the troublemaker.

There's more to your children than who they are today. Focus on your children's potential and on how much they've grown so far. Look for the best in your children, and refuse to label them in your mind. Even positive labels can have negative results. They can put your children on pedestals they're bound to fall off. View your children as God does, through eyes of love, always looking for the best.

look

> *Be sincere in your love for others. Hate everything that is evil and hold tight to everything that is good.*
>
> **Romans 12:9** CEV

≫ If you have nicknames for your children, review them carefully. Make sure they are positive and that your children enjoy it when you use them.

#62

Ask Questions

Little keys can open big locks. Simple words can express great thoughts.

William Arthur Ward

ask

Every mom has an opportunity to become an explorer searching for the hidden treasure God has placed in each of her children. A question is a key to help you unlock those riches and to help you better love and understand each child. Each child has a unique lock. Different questions will open different treasures within them.

In quiet moments during carpools, at bedtime, after school, or around the kitchen table, ask your children what they think, feel, hope, and believe to be true. Discuss their dreams and fears. Ask them what they'd like to ask you. Every new day offers a chance for discovery.

≫ The next time your children are facing emotionally tough times, ask God for wisdom in knowing what questions to ask and how to ask them.

#63

Foster Frugality

Money is a tool, not a toy. You can put your children on the road to becoming more financially responsible adults by showing them how far a dollar can stretch, with a little self-control and planning.

Acquaint your children with the benefits of shopping at secondhand stores and garage sales. Get your children in the habit of turning off lights when they leave a room and turning off the water when brushing their teeth. Introduce your children to the benefits of using public transportation. Shop out of necessity, not boredom. Model how to be thankful to God for what you have.

frugal

> *Keep your lives free from the love of money, and be satisfied with what you have.*
>
> Hebrews 13:5 NCV

>> Make a family game out of clipping coupons. Take the money you save on the grocery bill and put it toward a family vacation.

decide

101 ways to

discuss

rest

read

sing

be a great mom

share

imagine

enjoy

#64

Drop a Note

> *I write you letters by the thousands in my thoughts.*
>
> Ludwig van Beethoven

note

With e-mail, cell phones, and instant messaging, handwritten letters are almost a thing of the past. Yet there's a special joy in having a permanent record that expresses how much someone cares for you. That's one reason why God gave you the Bible. You can refer to what he's written to you over and over again, basking anew in God's love for you.

Give your children the gift of a love letter from Mom. Tape a card to the bathroom mirror. Put a note in their lunchboxes. Tuck a message into their coat pockets. All you need is a pencil, a piece of paper, and your heartfelt words.

≫ Write each of your children a note mentioning one reason why you're glad God chose you to be their mom. Place the notes on their pillows.

#65

Compliment Qualities, Not Just Accomplishments

As a mom, you're more than what you do. You may be a cook, a nurse, and a counselor, but most important, you're a one-of-a-kind child of God with a unique personality and place in history.

Your children are designed the same way. Throughout their lives, people may judge your children's value based on what they accomplish. As a mom, you know their true, eternal value is found in who they are, not what they do. Go ahead and congratulate your children on their successes in life. And take time to applaud their quieter success stories, stories of their success in practicing such qualities as patience, honesty, humility, and compassion.

compliment

People judge by outward appearance, but the LORD looks at a person's thoughts and intentions.

1 Samuel 16:7 NLT

>> Today, compliment each of your children on one of the godlike qualities of the heart that is evident in his or her life.

#66

Make Sick Days Fun

> *The best things you can give children, next to good habits, are good memories.*
>
> Sydney J. Harris

fun

Being sick isn't fun. A great mom can turn even sick days into happy memories. The key is preparing for them before they happen.

Along with having all of the basic medicinal aids on hand (children's cold medication, pain reliever, adhesive bandages, and syrup of ipecac), create a get-well-quick box. Fill it with inexpensive toys from garage sales or clearance bins. Choose amusements that are quiet and soothing in nature, such as puzzles, books, and games that children can enjoy by themselves. Keep the box hidden, and bring it out only when your child has to spend the day in bed.

≫ Pick up a few child-friendly videos or DVDs from the pre-viewed sale section of your local video store to be viewed only when your children are ill.

#67

Check Out the Bible Together

God has written a love letter to you and your children. This love letter is called the Bible. Within that letter, your heavenly Father provides guidelines for successful living, encouragement for tough times, and a glimpse into your eternal home. This amazing letter can change your mind and heart.

Depending on your children's ages, you may want to begin reading a book of children's Bible stories together. First find the story you're reading in your own Bible so that you can understand and share with your children the story's background. Discuss how the choices the people in the story made would be similar, or different, from your own.

Bible

Where two or three are gathered together in My name, I am there in the midst of them.

Matthew 18:20
NKJV

>> Before you read together with your children, take turns opening the time in prayer. Ask God to help you understand and apply what you read.

#68

Set Limits

When home is ruled according to God's Word, angels might be asked to stay with us, and they would not find themselves out of their element.

Charles Haddon Spurgeon

limits

Love sets limits. God gave the children of Israel rules. He knew that if they followed the Ten Commandments, the Israelites would lead happier, holier lives.

A great mom wants the same for her children and is diligent in setting loving limits to help achieve that end. She views limits as a way of encouraging her children toward accepting greater responsibility. She reviews her children's limits regularly, and she makes sure they're appropriate for their age and maturity level. She also provides a good example by living within the limits that God has set in the Bible for her and for all his people.

≫ Write down your family's rules in a notebook. That way, there won't be any arguments over what the limits actually are.

#69

Discipline Promptly

discipline

Back in the days of black-and-white television, when Mom wore pearls to clean the oven and she and Dad slept in separate twin beds, the most dreaded words a child could hear Mom say were, "Wait 'til your father gets home!" As entertainment goes, that may have been fine. However, when it comes to discipline, *now* is more effective than *later*.

The younger the child, the more important it is to discipline promptly. This helps children better connect your response to their inappropriate actions. Discuss with your spouse how you're going to discipline your children, so your response can be both consistent and prompt.

> *If you refuse to discipline your children, it proves you don't love them; if you love your children, you will be prompt to discipline them.*
>
> Proverbs 13:24 NLT

≫ When prompt discipline is required, begin by asking your children why they believe they're in trouble. Ask them how they could have made a better choice.

#70

Help Children Find Their Niche

> *A child is not a vase to be filled, but a fire to be lit.*
>
> François Rabelais

niche

God has a unique place in the world that only your children can fill. By growing up in your home, your children fill one corner of that niche. But there is so much more God wants them to be and do.

Your children's niches may be very different from your own. Invite your children to try activities you love, but also those removed from your interests and expertise. Encourage hobbies that build on their talents. Offer a variety of opportunities in the areas of sports, arts, sciences, and charities. Help your children search for purpose, as well as happiness, in life.

≫ If your children are interested in a certain profession, arrange for them to shadow someone with this job for a few hours to see what the work would really be like.

#71

Watch a Plant Grow

Whether you are a mom with a bona fide green thumb or you are a mom whose horticultural talents lean more toward tending silk, you can help plant a seed of faith in your children by watching a plant grow. As a visual aid, even a backyard weed will do.

Study the plant with your children over a period of time. Watch how it grows and changes with the seasons. Note how dependent it is on elements beyond its control. Look for similarities and differences between plants of the same family. Discuss God's creativity and care with your children, and tie in biblical principles that you can relate back to the plant.

plant

> *God gives such beauty to everything that grows in the fields, even though it is here today and thrown into a fire tomorrow. He will surely do even more for you!*
>
> Matthew 6:30 CEV

≫ When you read a Bible verse that mentions plants, draw a flower next to it. Use it as a reminder to talk about the verse with your children.

#72

Deal with Conflict

> *Peace is not the absence of conflict from life, but the ability to cope with it.*
>
> Author Unknown

conflict

Anytime there's conflict between you and your children, you and your spouse, or one sibling and another, face it head-on. Dealing with conflict as soon as possible will keep the lines of communication open and keep your love for each other growing.

When conflict erupts, stop what you're doing. If anger threatens to interfere with communication, spend a few minutes alone with God. Take turns talking and listening. Use positive, kind words, even when discussing difficult, emotion-filled problems. Get to the heart of hurt feelings. Ask God's help in the healing. Offer apologies. Make amends. Reconcile and forgive.

≫ When your children hurt each other's feelings, wait until they discuss and resolve the conflict before asking for apologies.

#73

Play by the Rules

rules

As a mom, you set up many of the rules you expect your children to live by in your home. You decide how many hours of television they can watch, what food they can snack on, and how clean their rooms have to be.

How do your expectations for your children compare with those you have for yourself? The more self-control and discipline you demonstrate in your own life, the better example your children will have to follow—and the more balanced life you'll live as a woman of God. Review the rules you try to live by, and consider how well you're living up to them.

> *To your knowledge, add self-control; and to your self-control, add patience; and to your patience, add service for God.*
>
> 2 Peter 1:6 NCV

≫ Write down the rules you believe God wants you to live by. Choose one area you struggle with. For the next month, ask God to help you improve in it.

#74

Take an After-School Break

> *The training of children is a profession where we must know how to lose time in order to gain it.*
>
> Jean F. Rousseau

break

After a busy day at work, most adults long for time to relax, regroup, and unwind before facing whatever tasks still lie ahead of them before bedtime. After a busy day at school, your children need the very same thing.

When children arrive home, put aside for at least a half-hour any homework, household chores, or disciplinary issues you want to address. Offer your children a snack. Sit and chat, if they're in the mood. Let them relax by burning off some energy outdoors. If possible, relax while they relax. Then you can all get back to work together when the break is over.

>> Set a timer or alarm clock to signal when the break is over. When it rings, keep your own attitude toward work positive, which will encourage your children to do the same.

#75

Make the Most of Carpools

Carpools can help you save gas, connect with other families, and make good use of your time. They can also give you the opportunity to share God's love with your children's friends.

Love every child well by greeting them warmly and making eye contact. Take care of them physically by making sure they are buckled safely in their seats. Pay as close attention to what children are talking about as you pay to watching the road. Ask questions, but be sensitive in knowing when to speak and when to simply listen. Let your car become more than transportation. Turn it into a safe, nurturing haven.

pools

I try to find common ground with everyone so that I might bring them to Christ.

1 Corinthians 9:22
NLT

≫ As each child gets into your car and buckles up, use that brief time to pray silently for him or her.

#76

Have Regular Checkups

*Take care of
your health,
that it may serve
you to serve God.*

Saint Francis de
Sales

checkup

One way you love your children is by taking care of their physical needs. Another way is by taking care of your own. Eating a balanced diet, along with getting enough sleep and exercise, is important. But even a healthy lifestyle can't guarantee a healthy life.

Have an annual checkup with both your family physician and your gynecologist. Follow their advice. Don't hesitate to ask questions you may have about how your body is changing as you age. And make an interim appointment if something just doesn't feel right. Becoming a healthier mom will help you be a better mom.

≫ If you're over forty, check to make sure you've had a mammogram in the last year. If not, schedule one.

#77

Put Work Away

The saying "a woman's work is never done" is true, at least until you find yourself at home in heaven. The laundry you folded today will be dirty again tomorrow. Your family will be hungry for dinner, no matter how well you fed them for breakfast.

Great moms are hard workers. That's simply part of the job description. But great moms also know when to put work away, both mentally and physically, and simply enjoy being with their family. When life is at its busiest, take regular breaks to play with your children. It'll reassure them they're more important than your to-do list.

work

> *Anyone who enters God's rest will rest from his work as God did.*
>
> Hebrews 4:10 NCV

≫ Schedule a family workday, and then surprise your children by doing something special together instead. Explain that work is important but that your favorite—and most important—job is being their mom.

#78

Look for God Together

> *The believer goes through life calmly and peacefully, with profound joy — like a child, hand in hand with his mother.*
>
> Charles de Foucauld

look

From the moment of their birth, your children search for evidence of your love. They look for it in your smile, your words, your touch, and your care. As children of God, you and your children are looking for the same thing from your heavenly Father. Since God is Spirit, not flesh, discerning his love requires a different approach.

Don't let a day go by without bringing up his name. Pray aloud as a family. Look for how God brings good out of difficult circumstances. Share what God's teaching you. At the same time, allow your children's simple faith to teach you a spiritual lesson or two.

≫ At the dinner table tonight, have each person share one way in which he or she experienced God's love today. As a family, thank God for what's shared.

#79

Regulate Internet Use

Today, many children can outsurf their moms when it comes to maneuvering their way around the Internet. Chat rooms, instant messaging, and e-mails have changed the way children communicate, while the Web has changed the way they search for information.

As a mom who cares about guarding your children's minds and hearts, you need to take a few precautions concerning Internet use. Talk to your children about how valuable, and vulnerable, their minds are. Block access to adult sites. Keep the computer in a common area visible to the whole family. Prohibit late-night use. Help your children honor God by the way they surf.

regulate

> *Keep your minds on whatever is true, pure, right, holy, friendly, and proper. Don't ever stop thinking about what is truly worthwhile and worthy of praise.*
>
> Philippians 4:8 CEV

>> Regularly open the history folder on your browser to make sure your children are not visiting any sites you'd rather keep off-limits.

give

101 ways to

congratulate

create

provide

discipline

be a great mom

invite

study

forgive

#80

Just Say "Yes"

> Busyness is the enemy of spirituality . . . It is filling our time with our own actions instead of paying attention to God's actions. It is taking charge.
>
> Eugene Peterson

yes

Saying yes to motherhood means making some major commitments for the next eighteen-plus years. To fulfill the responsibilities of this yes, you need to know what to say no to.

Every day, ask God for wisdom in knowing where to commit your limited time and energy. Ask him to help you weigh potential responsibilities against the ones you've already accepted as a mom. Anytime you find yourself struggling to be the mom you want to be, reassess your schedule, making necessary changes as your children mature. Allow God to help you say yes to the joy motherhood brings.

≫ The next time you're asked to commit your time to something, respond by saying, "I'll let you know tomorrow." Pray and evaluate carefully before answering.

#81

Live Your Own Life

As a child, you probably had dreams that never came true. Perhaps you wanted to take karate, play the tuba, or be a model. Having children of your own may feel like a second chance to fulfill those dreams. But God has given your children only one life to live, their own.

When encouraging your children along the road of life, carefully examine the direction you're pointing them. Ask yourself if that direction is God's or if it is simply the one you would most like your children to pursue. Focus more on helping your children follow God's plans for their lives rather than your plan.

live

> *Our lives get in step with God and all others by letting him set the pace, not by proudly or anxiously trying to run the parade.*
>
> **Romans 3:28** MSG

≫ Recall your favorite childhood dreams. Ask God if any of them are still worth pursuing—through your own life, not through your children's.

#82

Battle Boredom with Creativity

> *Boredom acts as an initiator of originality by pushing me into new activities or new thoughts.*
>
> Hugh Prather

battle

"I'm bored" is a common complaint from children of all ages. However, boredom is more a state of mind than a lack of opportunity.

Help your children battle boredom by living out the truth that life is a daily adventure. Keep supplies on hand to get those creative juices flowing. Supplies could include construction paper, poster board, crayons, paint, stickers, and glue sticks. Add books that include crafts, puzzles, and games to your library. Instead of letting your children watch television, have them create their own show and act it out in front of the family. Maybe you'll even get a cameo role.

>> When socks are outgrown or wearing out, wash and save them. Help your children use buttons, yarn, safety pins, and iron-on patches to create puppets. Then let the show begin.

#83

Watch How You Drive

Your children begin learning how to drive long before they ever get behind the wheel. Every time they're passengers in your car, they're also students.

Whether you're picking your children up from school or picking up dinner at the drive-through, remember that your children are picking up driving tips and techniques, as well as attitudes. Exceeding the speed limit, turning without signaling, following other drivers too closely, and only slowing at stop signs teaches them that it's okay to break laws as long as they don't get caught. Treat other drivers, the law, and your vehicle the way you hope your children will in the future.

drive

Remind your people to submit to the government and its officers. They should be obedient, always ready to do what is good.

Titus 3:1 NLT

≫ Always have your children remove trash and belongings from the car when you arrive home. Explain how caring for what God gives you is a way of honoring him.

#84

Snuggle and Cuddle

> *The first step in personhood is to allow ourselves to be loved. To know ourselves loved is to have the depths of our own capacity to love opened up.*
>
> John Main

cuddle

Jesus was a hands-on kind of person. He touched lepers, washed his companions' feet, and placed his hands on children in blessing. Though Jesus' words alone could work miracles, his touch helped him connect on a more personal level with individuals.

Touching your children in loving and playful ways helps you connect with them more deeply. Tousle their hair. Tickle their toes. Wipe away their tears. Be generous with your hugs and kisses. Also, cuddle with your spouse in front of them. How you treat your family physically can be an indicator of how they'll treat the people they love in the future.

≫ If your children are embarrassed by affection shown in public, offer an alternative. Agree on a wink or a pat on the shoulder as your secret code for "I love you."

#85

Treat Your Children as Individuals

Parenting is like a potluck. You never know what you're going to get. God has a unique recipe for every child. Part of being a great mom is deciphering these physical, emotional, and mental recipes as the years go by.

It takes more thought, prayer, creativity, and effort on your part to respond to your children as individuals in areas such as discipline, affirmation, and affection, but it's worth it. Study your children. Be willing to try parenting techniques that may not come naturally to you. Learn to enjoy the unique flavor each one of your children brings to life.

individual

> *Don't be afraid, I've redeemed you. I've called your name. You're mine.*
>
> Isaiah 43:1 MSG

>> Pick up a book on personality types or love languages at your local bookstore. See what you can decipher about each of your children's "recipes" by reading it.

#86

Picnic Year-Round

> *Joy is the echo of God's life in us.*
>
> Joseph Marmion

picnic

Feeding your family is a huge job. Every year, you probably make close to a thousand meals, not including snacks. You can save time and money, as well as make some great memories, by shaking up your familiar routine with a picnic.

All you need is an old tablecloth (or blanket), some paper plates and plasticware, and finger food. Simple sandwiches, leftover chicken, or a buffet of cold cuts, fruit, cheese, and crackers will do. If weather prevents you from eating outside, picnic by the fireplace, in the family room while watching a movie, or even in a large walk-in closet by flashlight. Use your imagination and enjoy.

≫ Keep the picnic cleanup as easy as the preparation. Officially end each picnic by having each person wash, dry, and put away his or her own plasticware.

#87

Cheer Your Favorite Team

Teamwork is important, whether you're playing baseball, running relay races, or raising a family. Watching sporting events with your children can provide you with a visual aid to jump-start discussions on the benefits of teamwork and on how to handle both victory and defeat.

Attending games your children are participating in should be a high priority. Watch a variety of professional and local sporting events as a family. Cheer together. Talk about sportsmanship, adherence to the rules, and persever-ance. Simple comments and questions in light of what you witness together can instill lifelong lessons.

cheer

Encourage one another and build each other up, just as in fact you are doing.

1 Thessalonians 5:11
NIV

≫ Watch a sporting event on television as a family, choosing a family team and wearing the team's colors. Chat afterward about what you learned.

#88

Give Handmade Gifts

> God has given us
> two hands — one for
> receiving and the
> other for giving.
>
> Billy Graham

gifts

Moms know firsthand the joy of receiving handmade gifts. Whether it's a drawing for the refrigerator or a clay handprint from school, the first gifts children give are made by hand.

Continuing this tradition as children mature helps nurture creativity and frugality. Furthermore, it helps instill a greater appreciation for the gift of time, as opposed to money. Keep gift-friendly supplies on hand: wrapping paper, ribbon, used greeting cards, felt, clay, cardboard, earring findings, and so forth. Let your children know that the gift closet is ready whenever they want to express their love, and that cleaning up afterward is always a gift you love to receive.

>> This Christmas, ask each person to make a handmade gift for every member of the family. Save opening them until the very end of your celebration.

#89

Make Allowances for Allowances

Raising your children to be responsible adults includes teaching them how to handle money in a God-honoring way. An allowance is a great tool to help achieve this goal.

At what age your children start receiving an allowance, and how much you decide to give, is up to you. However, get your children in the habit of putting 10 percent of what they receive into savings and giving 10 percent to your church or a charitable organization. (Make sure you're also teaching by example!) Part of the learning process includes making mistakes. Allow the consequences of their mistakes to speak louder than your words.

allowance

> *The blessing of the LORD makes a person rich, and he adds no sorrow with it.*
>
> Proverbs 10:22 NLT

≫ When your children need more money than they have, don't offer an advance on their allowance, which teaches them to live on credit. Instead, offer cash for an extra chore.

#90

Be a Memory-Maker

> *You will find as you look back upon your life that the moments when you have really lived are the moments when you have done things in the spirit of love.*
>
> Henry Drummond

Some of life's most cherished memories are spontaneous gifts from God—the perfect sunset, a chance encounter with an old friend, the first time your child says "I love you." Moms can be memory-makers too.

The surest way to be a memory-maker is to be authentic, consistent, and transparent with your love. Let your words, your touch, and your actions fully express your emotions. Care for the handmade gifts and school memorabilia you receive. Honor existing family memories by keeping a family scrapbook or photo album. Daily ask God to help you be a mom who makes lasting memories by loving her children well.

≫ Think about your happiest childhood memory. Consider what makes it so memorable. Put what you learn to use to help make a memorable moment for your own children.

#91

Learn a New Language

When your children are small, learning a new language comes easily. They can imitate your words and speech patterns in just a few short years. As they age, their ability to learn a new language and accurately imitate foreign sounds becomes much more difficult.

Give your children a head start in mastering a foreign tongue—and gaining a broader world-view—by introducing them to a variety of languages while they're young. Sing along with songs from around the world. Learn basic words or phrases such as *hello, good-bye, please*, and *thank you* in several languages, and use them anytime you eat a meal indigenous to that country.

learn

Intelligent people are always open to new ideas. In fact, they look for them.

Proverbs 18:15
NLT

≫ If your children are old enough to read, check out a foreign family film subtitled in English. Learn at least one new foreign phrase as you watch it together.

#92

Have a Just-Because Party

> *All of our life is a celebration for us.*
>
> Clement of Alexandria

party

Throughout the Old Testament, God encouraged his people to remember his goodness toward them. He asked them to celebrate what he'd done with feasts and merrymaking.

You can carry on a version of this Old Testament tradition by throwing a party—just because God loves you. When God answers a heartfelt prayer, blesses your family in an unexpected way, or even when life is hard and you simply need a reminder of God's faithfulness, celebrate with balloons, streamers, cake, and ice cream—whatever puts you in a festive mood. Begin with a prayer and a song of thanksgiving. Then party, just because.

≫ Take a photo of your just-because party. Put it in a scrapbook along with a thank-you note to God for what he did to inspire the celebration.

#93
Relish Responsibility

Every task you face as a mom, from changing diapers to teaching your children about God, is an awesome responsibility. Some jobs may seem more monumental than others. But how well you handle each one of your responsibilities demonstrates how well you're honoring God as a parent.

Relish the responsibilities of motherhood. Picture each difficult task as a precious gift you're extending to God with open arms. Remind yourself of the eternal value of everything you do for and with your children. Strive for excellence, and yet rest in God's promise of grace and forgiveness whenever you fail to reach your goal.

relish

> *In all the work you are doing, work the best you can. Work as if you were doing it for the Lord, not for people.*
>
> Colossians 3:23 NCV

>> Today, as you're tackling any parenting responsibility that isn't particularly enjoyable, picture God watching you and smiling as you work to the very best of your ability.

#94

Rely on God

> *Young mother, your motherhood is in God's sight a holier and a more blessed thing than you know.*
>
> Andrew Murray

rely

Motherhood takes effort. Good moms don't become great moms simply by striving to be more organized, more creative, and more self-disciplined. They become great by relying on God and not solely on themselves.

Begin each new day by turning to God. Humbly admit how much you need his strength, his wisdom, and his guidance to help you be the woman, and great mom, he created you to be. Ask him for help where you need it most. Thank him for how he demonstrates his love. Then look ahead with excitement, and be keenly aware of God's presence and participation in the day ahead.

>> Take a few moments to relax, close your eyes, and enjoy God's loving presence in your life.

#95

Tend Your Family Tree

How many people are in your family? Before you answer, remember that your family extends far beyond the number of people who sit around your dinner table. Parents, grandparents, aunts, uncles, cousins, in-laws, and many more people make up the typical family tree.

Keeping your family tree healthy takes a group effort. However, you're the only member of that group you're fully responsible for. Do your part. Keep lines of communication open. Work through conflict. Be generous with birthday cards, thank-you notes, and encouraging words. Speak positively about your relatives in front of your children, and pray for them regularly as a family.

tend

> *Whoever does not care for his own relatives, especially his own family members, has turned against the faith and is worse than someone who does not believe in God.*
>
> 1 Timothy 5:8 NCV

>> Today, call a family member you haven't spoken to in a while and let him or her know how much you care.

reassess

101 ways to

dream

act

touch

feed

be a great mom

comment

honor

rely

#96

Keep Tabs on Toys

> *Lives based on having are less free than lives based either on doing or on being.*
>
> William James

toys

Every member of the family—whether the member is your toddler with a new tricycle or your husband with a new sound system—enjoys getting a new toy. There is nothing wrong with enjoying, and acquiring, possessions, unless what you own begins to own you.

Help loosen the grip toys have on your family by shopping for specific items instead of simply looking for bargains. Give one perfect present for Christmas and birthdays instead of multiple useless trinkets that the recipient will use once and then forget. Wait before making impulse purchases. It's better to spend time returning to a store than to spend money foolishly.

>> Each time your children receive a new toy, encourage them to give away to charity a toy that they have outgrown.

#97

Start a Tradition

The traditions your family chooses to practice could end up being remembered and repeated for generations—a birthday cake for Jesus on Christmas Day, a balloon tied to the back of a child's chair to celebrate a special accomplishment, a heartfelt prayer spoken over your children every evening at bedtime.

Choose to begin traditions, or continue those from your own heritage, that reflect what you cherish most. Keep them simple. Traditions have a better chance of being passed on if they don't take a lot of time and effort. Talk about the meaning behind your traditions. Then invite your children to start some of their own.

start

This is the day the LORD has made; we will rejoice and be glad in it.

Psalm 118:24 NKJV

≫ Choose one way you'd like to honor God as a family. Start a new tradition that reflects your choice this week.

#98

Dance 'Til You Drop

> *In the child*
> *happiness dances.*
>
> John Paul Richter

dance

When David was bursting with gratitude to God for what he had done for the nation of Israel, David did more than praise God with his voice. He praised him with his feet by dancing in the streets.

Dancing can be great exercise, great fun, and a great expression of your thanks to God. It can also help your children become more aware of musical meter and rhythmic patterns, and it can prepare them for training their voices or mastering musical instruments in the future. Follow in David's footsteps. Put aside your own inhibitions, and join your children in a dance of joy today.

>> Spend a few minutes talking with your children about the good things God has done. Then turn on a lively worship song and dance together as a gift to God.

#99

Get Involved in Education

education

Your children spend a large part of their growing years in pursuit of an education. Good moms cheer their children along in this pursuit from the sidelines. Great moms run right alongside them.

If you've chosen to homeschool your children, support them outside of class by attending local conferences, connecting with other homeschool parents, and keeping in contact with your school district about changing laws and special opportunities. If your children are in public or private school, get to know your school board and staff. As your schedule allows, volunteer to help out in the classroom, and take time to pray for their teachers.

> *If you have good sense, instruction will help you to have even better sense. And if you live right, education will help you to know even more.*
>
> Proverbs 9:9 CEV

>> Skim your children's textbooks before they begin a new class so you can be better prepared to help them with homework and ask questions about what they're learning.

#100
Let Go As They Grow

> *There are two lasting bequests we can give our children: One is roots. The other is wings.*
>
> Hodding Carter Jr.

let go

A great mom is like a set of training wheels. She gives her children support as they learn how to balance their own lives. One day those training wheels will have to come off. Letting go isn't easy. Neither is watching your children wobble and skin their knees a few times before they're off on their own. Just remember, they're not alone.

God is always there, even when you can't be. Teaching your children to lean less and less on you will encourage them to lean more and more on God. Loosen your grip a bit each day. Letting children go will help them grow.

≫ Talk to God about one area you have trouble letting go of in your children's lives. Ask for God's strength and wisdom in knowing how to loosen your grip.

#101

Savor Every Stage

Though you'll always be a mom, how you mother your children will change as time goes by. Celebrate the change. Though saying good-bye to a time when you cradled your baby in your arms can be tough, it's the only way you can say hello to first steps, first words, first dates, and first grandchildren.

Make a conscious decision to enjoy every stage of motherhood. Ask God to help you grab hold of today and throw your whole heart into being a great mom. Savor each stage. Cherish each child. Treasure each memory. Being a mom is one of the greatest gifts you'll ever enjoy.

savor

> To everything there is a season, a time for every purpose under heaven.
>
> Ecclesiastes 3:1 NKJV

≫ Celebrate the season of motherhood you're in right now by telling God, and your children, what you love most about it.

Each day of our lives we make deposits in the memory banks of our children.

Charles R. Swindoll

The godly are showered with blessings.

Proverbs 10:6 NLT